# WORKBOOK

# CORNERSTONE POCKETS 1

## Mario Herrera   Barbara Hojel

PEARSON
Longman

**Cornerstone Pockets Workbook 1**

Copyright © by Pearson Education, Inc.
All rights reserved.
No part of this publication may be reproduced,
stored in a retrieval system, or transmitted
in any form or by any means, electronic, mechanical,
photocopying, recording, or otherwise,
without the prior permission of the publisher.

Pearson Education, 10 Bank Street, White Plains, NY 10606

Rhea Banker
Iris Candelaria
Nancy Flaggman
Yoko Mia Hirano
Louise Jennewine
Ed Lamprich
Christopher Leonowicz
Javier Montiel
Tracey Munz Cataldo
Susan Saslow

ISBN: 978-0-13-135904-8
ISBN: 0-13-135904-5

Printed in the United States of America
2 3 4 5–DHS–12 11 10 09 08

# Contents

| Unit 1 | My Classroom | 2 |
| Unit 2 | My Body | 10 |
| Unit 3 | My Toys | 18 |
| Unit 4 | My Family | 26 |
| Unit 5 | Our Pets | 34 |
| Unit 6 | My Clothes | 42 |
| Unit 7 | Party Food | 50 |
| Unit 8 | Around My Home | 58 |
| Unit 9 | Nature Around Us | 66 |

Puppet ................................................. 75

Certificate ............................................ 77

# UNIT 1 My Classroom

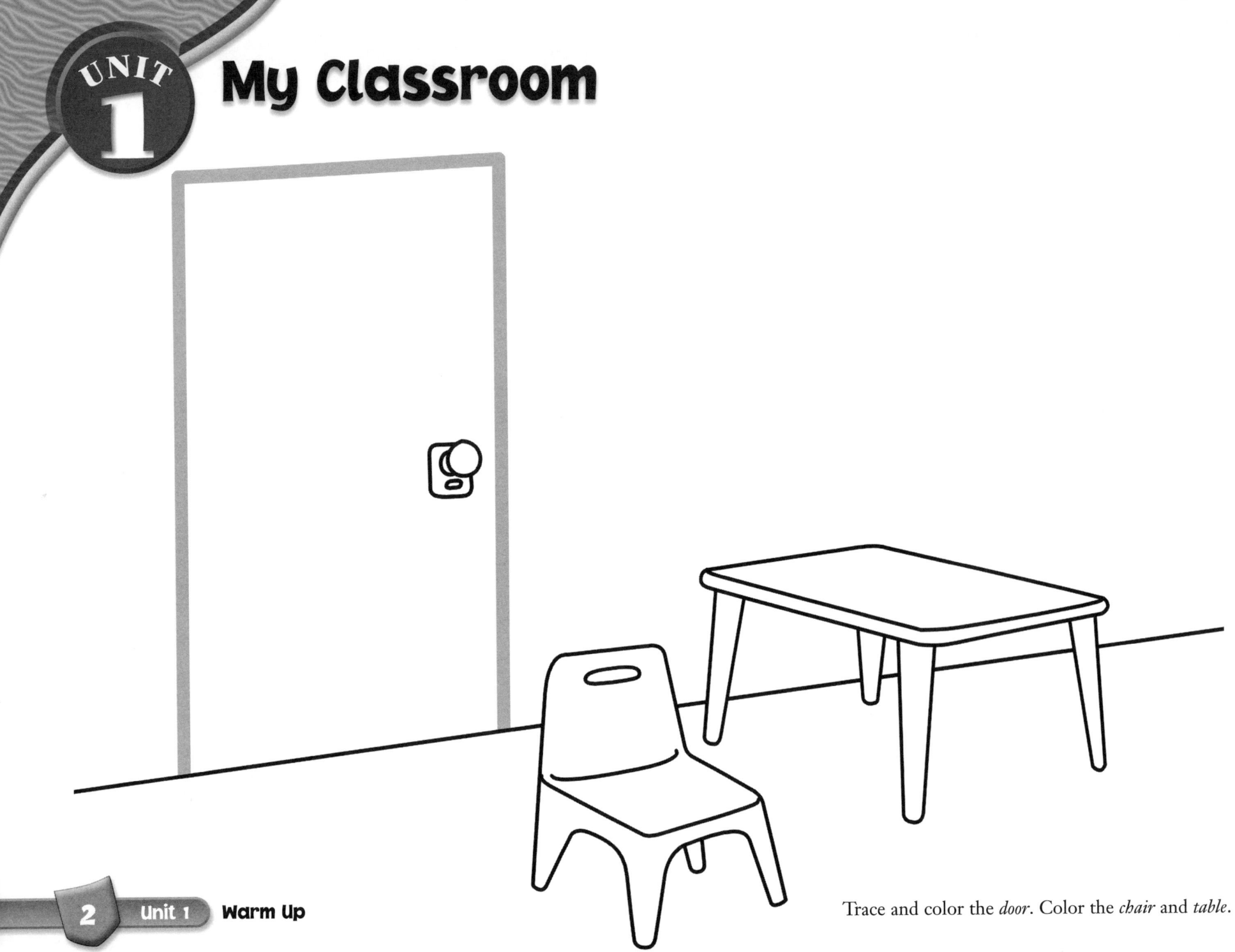

Unit 1 Warm Up

Trace and color the *door*. Color the *chair* and *table*.

Trace and color the *paper*. Color the *crayon* and *glue*.

Trace the *circle*. Find more *circles* and color them.

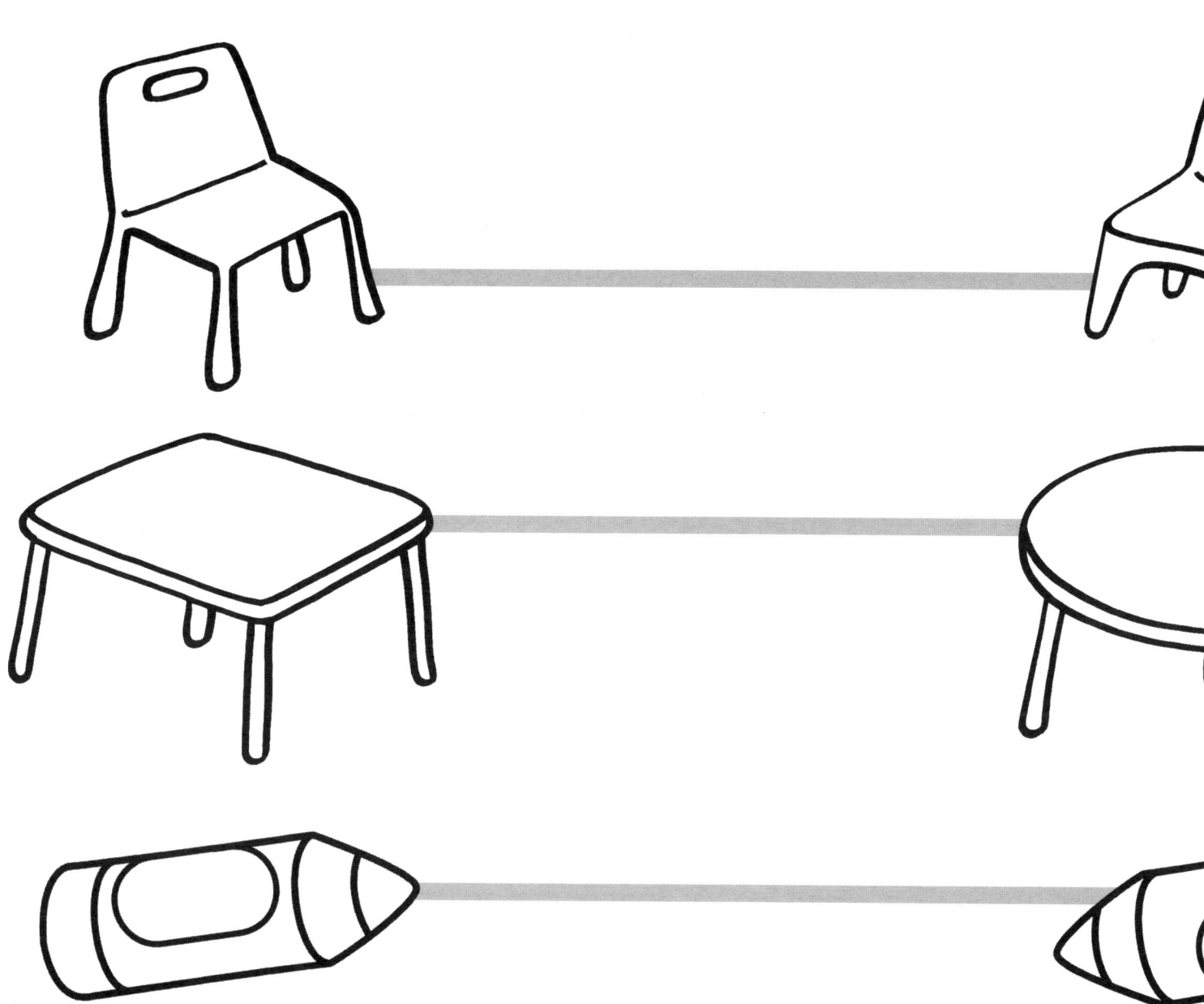

Trace the lines. Say.

Practice Unit 1  5

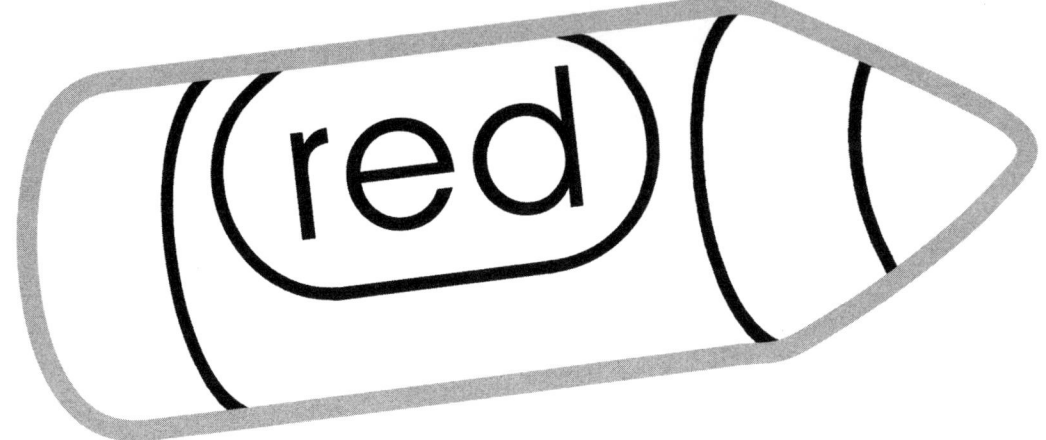

Unit 1 **Practice**

Trace the crayon and color.

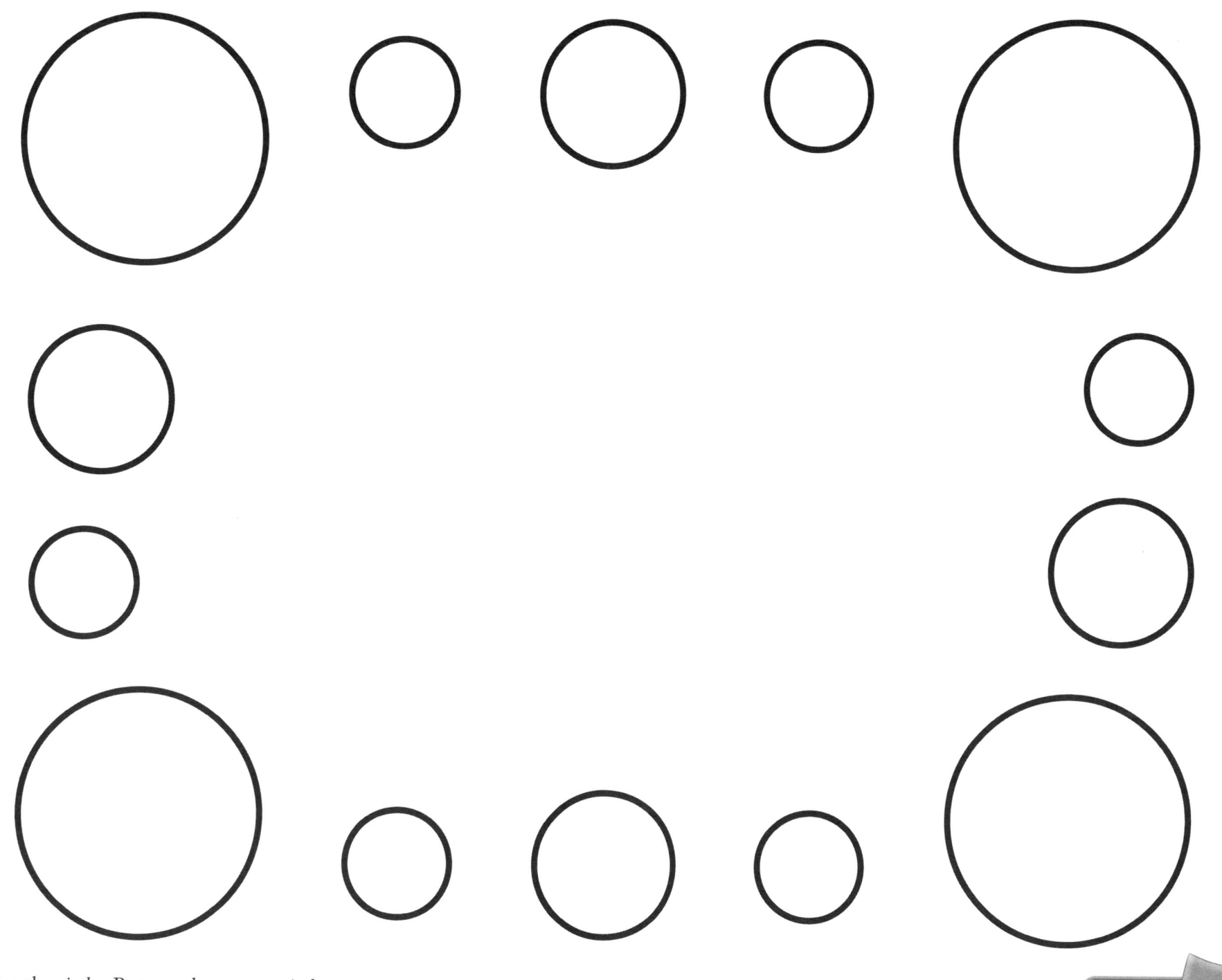

Color the *circles*. Paste or draw more *circles*.

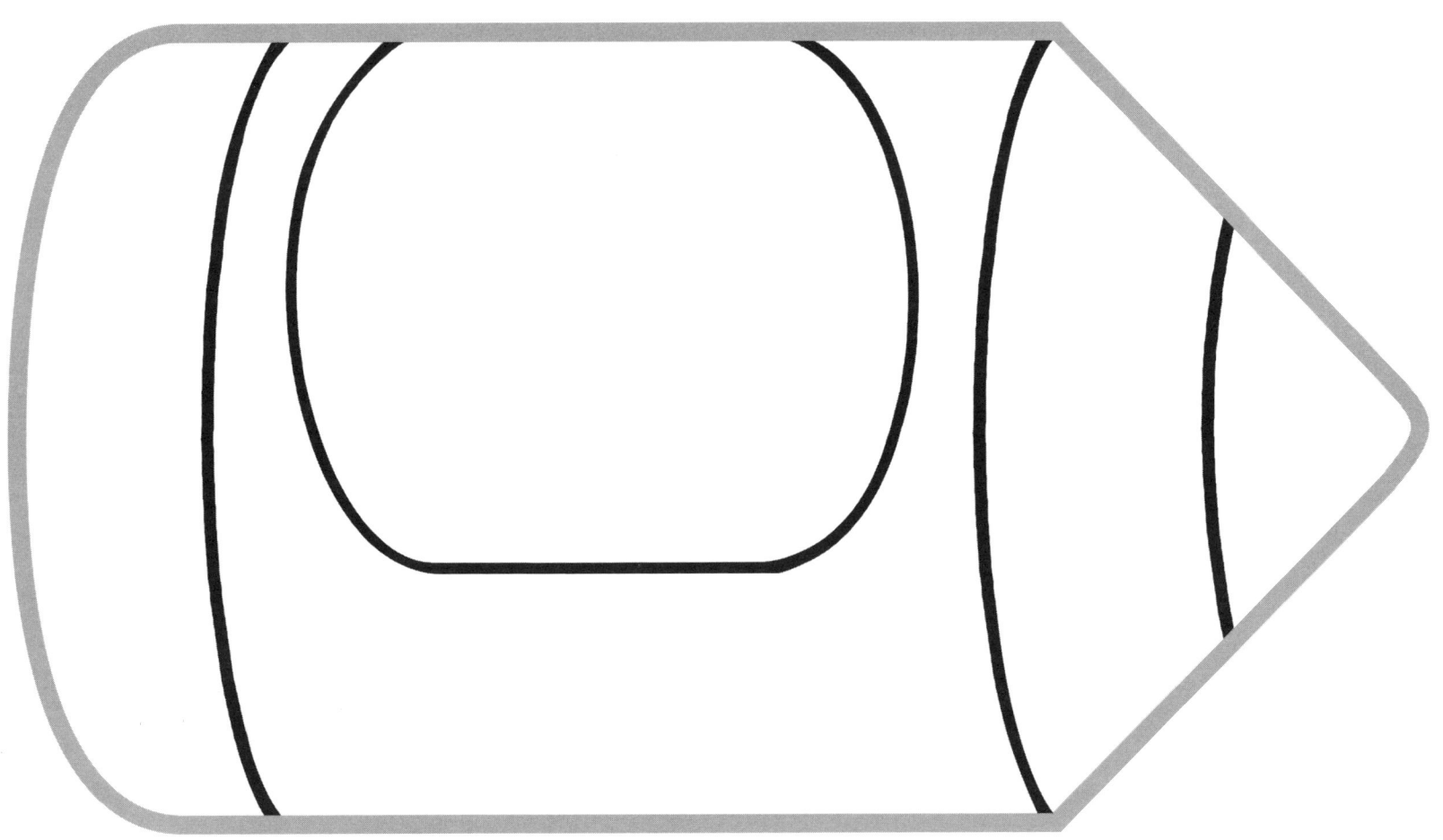

Trace the *crayon*. Glue paper or tissue on the *crayon*.

# My Classroom

Point to the items and say. Draw yourself in the classroom.

Assessment Unit 1

# UNIT 2 My Body

Trace the *mouth*, *nose*, and *eyes*. Color.

Trace the *arm*, *leg*, and *ear*. Color.

Presentation Unit 2 11

Trace the *circles* and color.

Trace and color.

Practice Unit 2

Trace the crayon and color.

Trace the lines to match the face parts. Match the *nose*.

Practice Unit 2 15

Glue yarn or sticks for the *arms* and *legs*. Point and say.

Point to the items and the body parts and say. Draw yourself.

# UNIT 3 My Toys

Trace and color the *boat*. Color the *game* and *doll*.

Trace and color the *teddy bear*. Color the *puppet* and *train*.

Trace the *square*. Color.

Trace the lines to the *boat* and *doll*.
Draw lines from the other children to the *train* and *teddy bear*.

Trace the crayon and color.

Trace and color the *squares* and *circles*. Draw another toy.

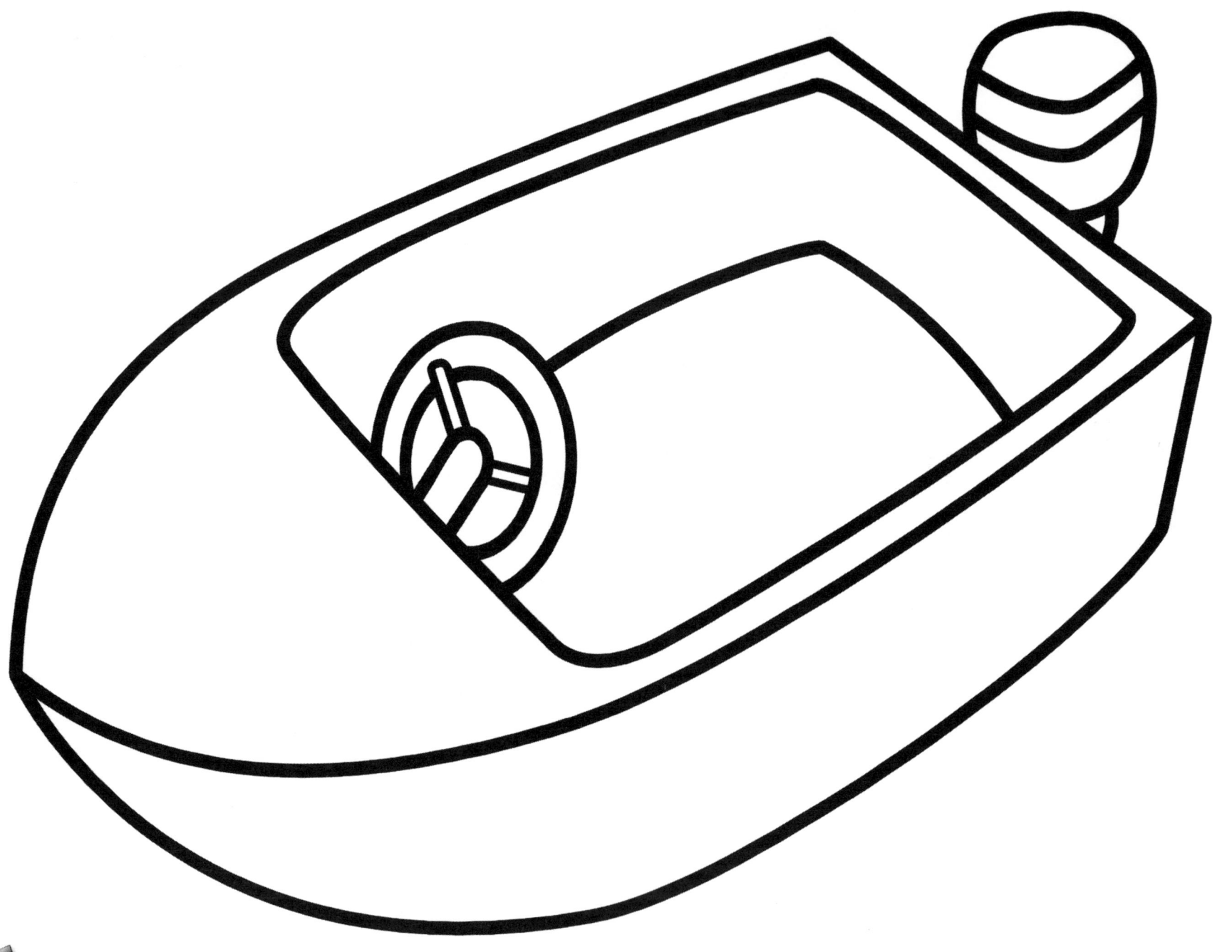

Glue paper or tissue on the *boat*.

# My Toys

Point to the items and say. Draw your favorite toy.

Assessment Unit 3

# UNIT 4 My Family

26 Unit 4 **Warm Up**

Trace and color the *baby*. Color the *mother*, *father*, and *brother*.

Trace and color the *sister*. Color the *grandfather* and *grandmother*.

Trace the *squares*. Color.

Trace the line from the *mother* to the *mother*. Draw lines between the other family members: *brother*, *sister*, *grandmother*.

**Practice** Unit 4

Trace the crayon and color.

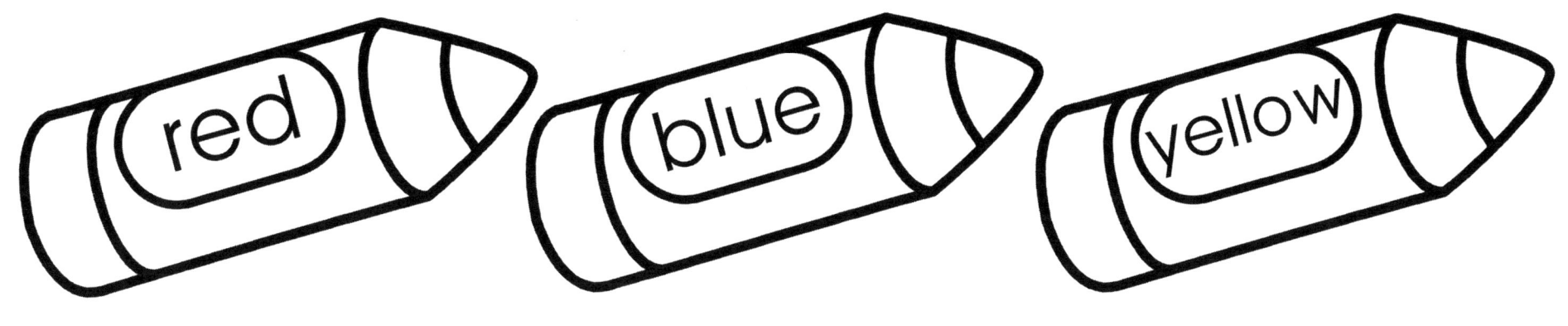

Color the crayons. Then color the items.

Trace the *squares*. Glue paper or tissue on the *squares*.

# My Family

Point to the items and say. Draw your family.

Assessment Unit 4

# UNIT 5 Our Pets

Trace and color the *fish*. Color the *rabbit* and *turtle*.

Trace and color the *dog*. Color the *cat* and *bird*.

Presentation  Unit 5  35

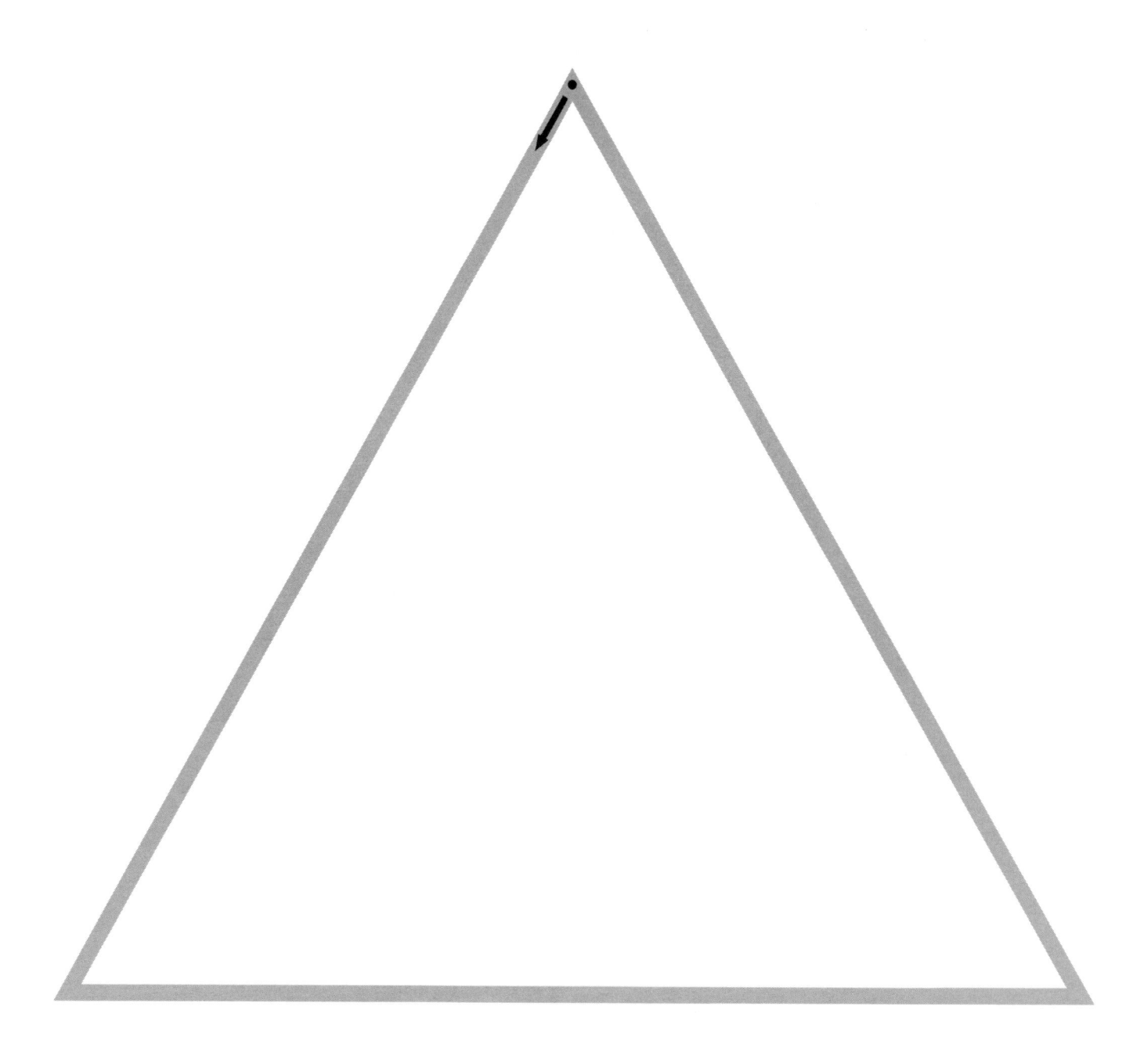

Trace the *triangle*. Glue paper or tissue on the *triangle*.

Trace the fish bowl. Draw and color a *fish* in the bowl.

Practice Unit 5 37

orange

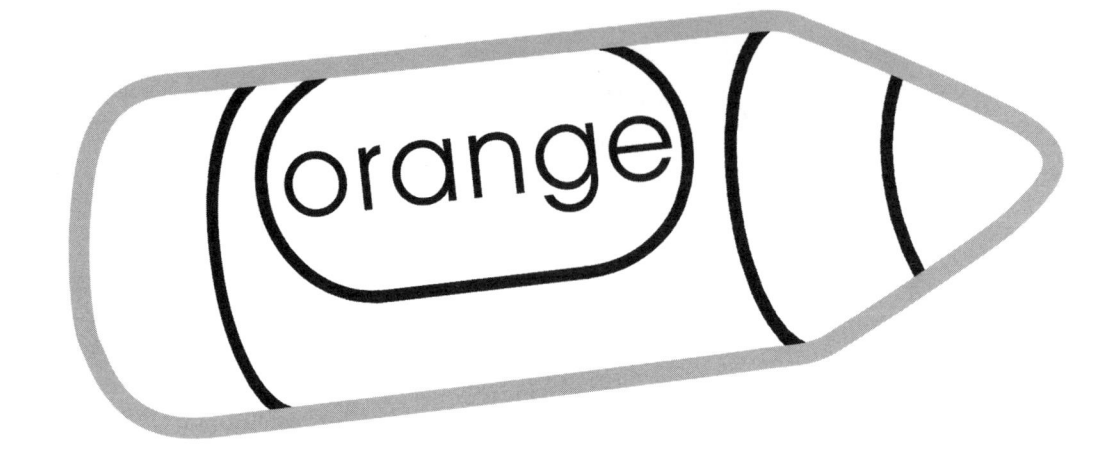

38 Unit 5 Practice

Trace the crayon and color.

Match the shapes. Color the shapes *red*, *blue*, *yellow*, *green*, and *orange*.

Practice Unit 5 39

Trace the carrot. Glue *orange* yarn or tissue on the carrot.

# Our Pets

Point to the items and animals and say. Draw your favorite pet.

Assessment  Unit 5  41

# UNIT 6 My Clothes

42 Unit 6 **Warm Up**

Trace and color the *dress*. Color the *pajamas* and *T-shirt*.

Trace and color the *pants*. Color the *shoes* and the *jacket*.

Presentation  Unit 6  43

Unit 6 Practice

Trace the *triangles* and color.

Trace the line from the boy to the *shoes*.
Draw lines from the other children to the clothes.

**Practice** Unit 6　45

purple

46 Unit 6 Practice

Trace the crayon and color.

Color and say. Draw the *shoes*.

Practice Unit 6  47

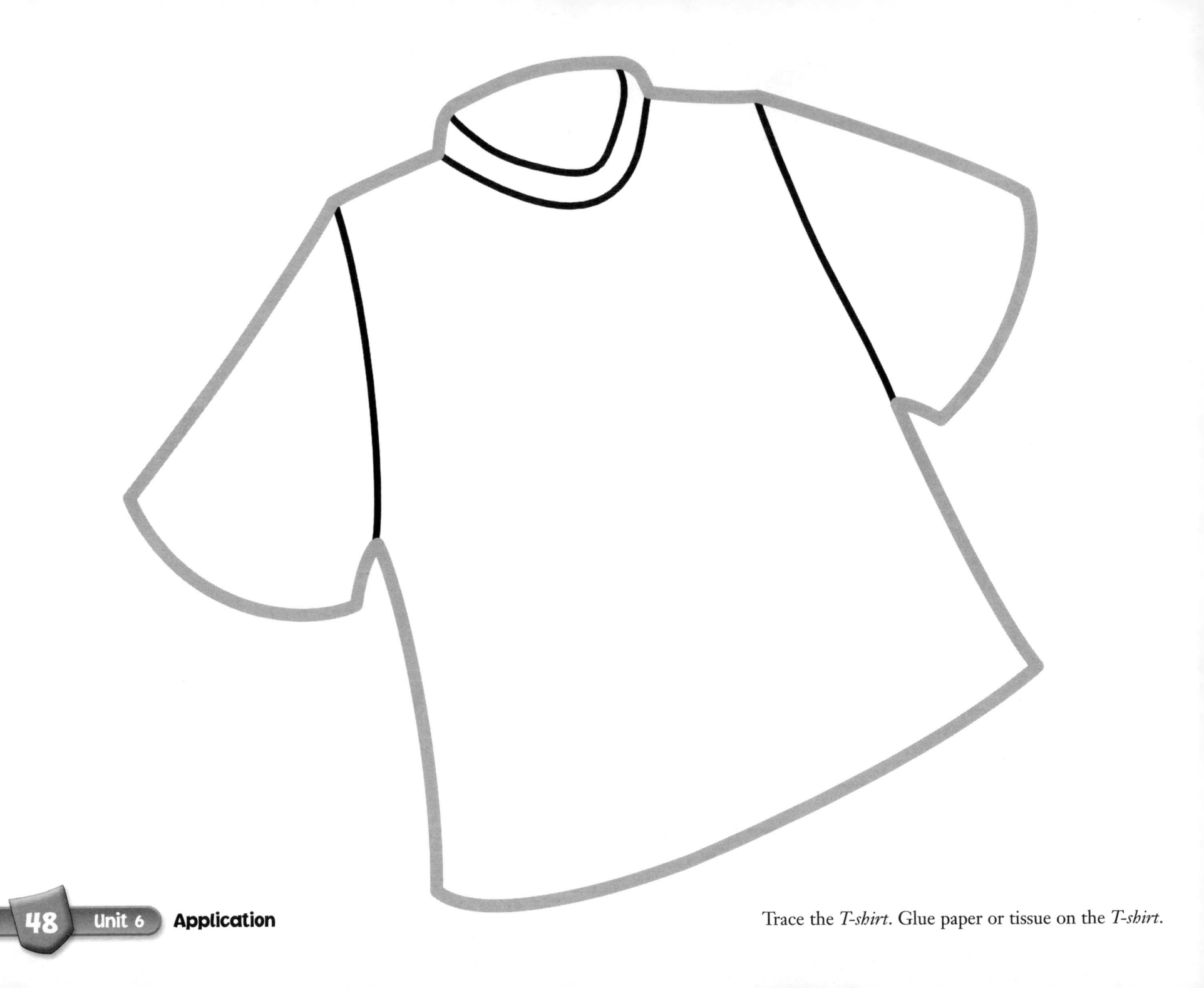

**48** Unit 6 **Application**

Trace the *T-shirt*. Glue paper or tissue on the *T-shirt*.

# My Clothes

Point to the items and say. Draw your favorite clothes.

Assessment  Unit 6

# UNIT 7 Party Food

50 Unit 7 **Warm Up**

Trace and color the *pizza*. Color the *cake* and the *orange juice*.

Trace and color the *lemonade*. Color the *sandwich* and the *ice cream*.

Presentation  Unit 7  51

52 Unit 7 **Presentation**

Trace the *rectangle*. Glue paper or tissue on the *rectangle*.

Trace the *rectangle*. Color the shapes and say.

pink

54 Unit 7 Practice

Trace the crayon and color.

Trace the *pizza* and *ice cream*. Color.

56 Unit 7 **Application**

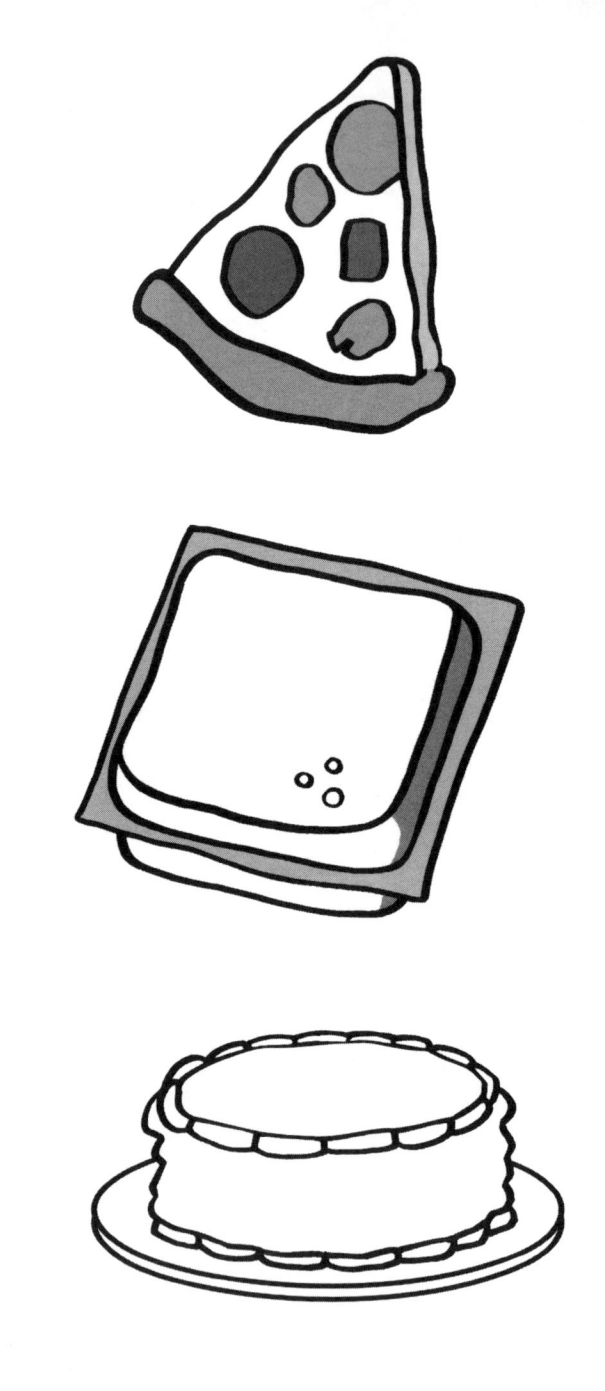

Draw a line from the shape to the food. Color.

# Party Food

Point to the items and say. Draw your favorite food.

**Assessment** Unit 7

# UNIT 8
# Around My Home

Trace and color the *apartments*. Color the *swings* and *park*.

Trace and color the *slide*. Color the *tricycle* and *store*.

60 Unit 8 Practice

Trace the *apartments*. Glue paper or tissue on the *apartments*.

Take a walk. Point and say what you see. Color.

Practice Unit 8 61

brown

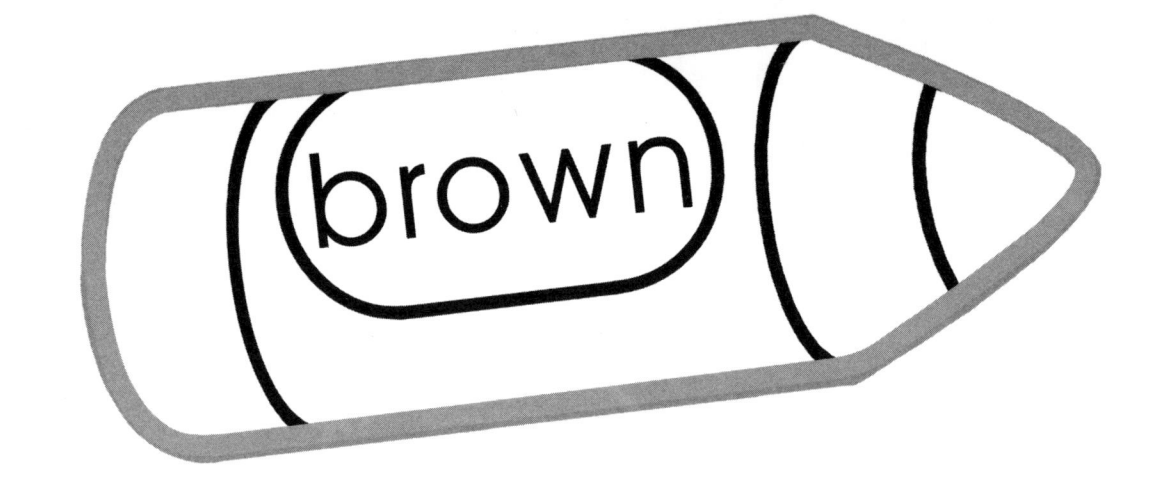

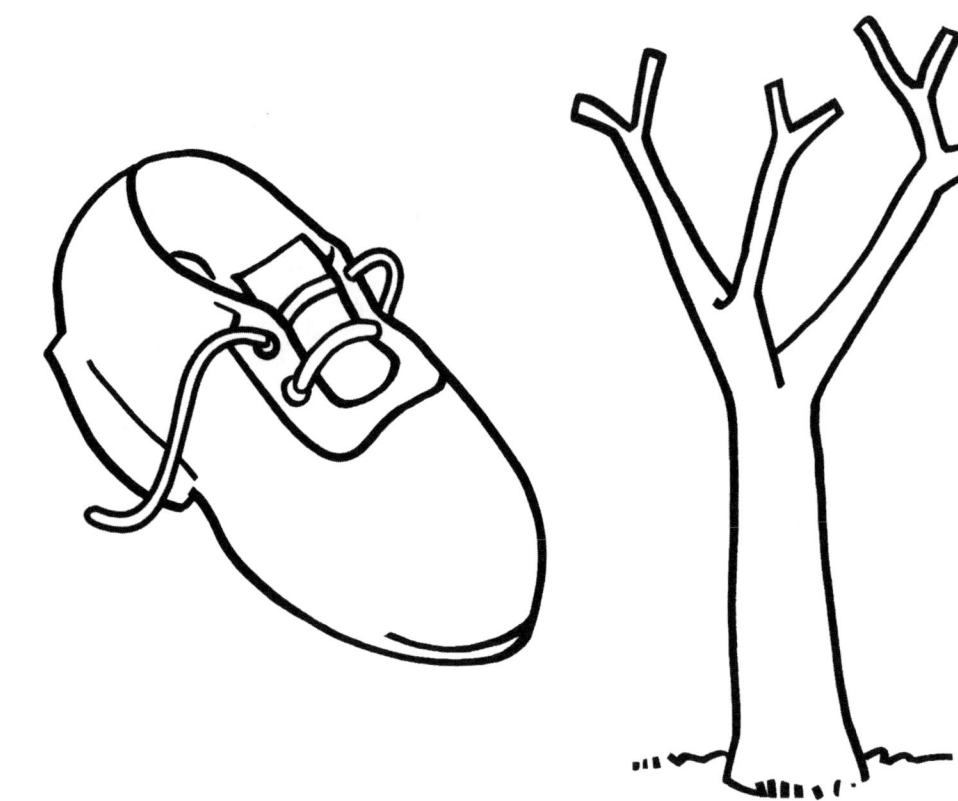

62 Unit 8 Practice

Trace the crayon and color.

Trace and draw lines to complete the *swings*. Color.

Unit 8  Application

Draw yourself on the slide. Color.

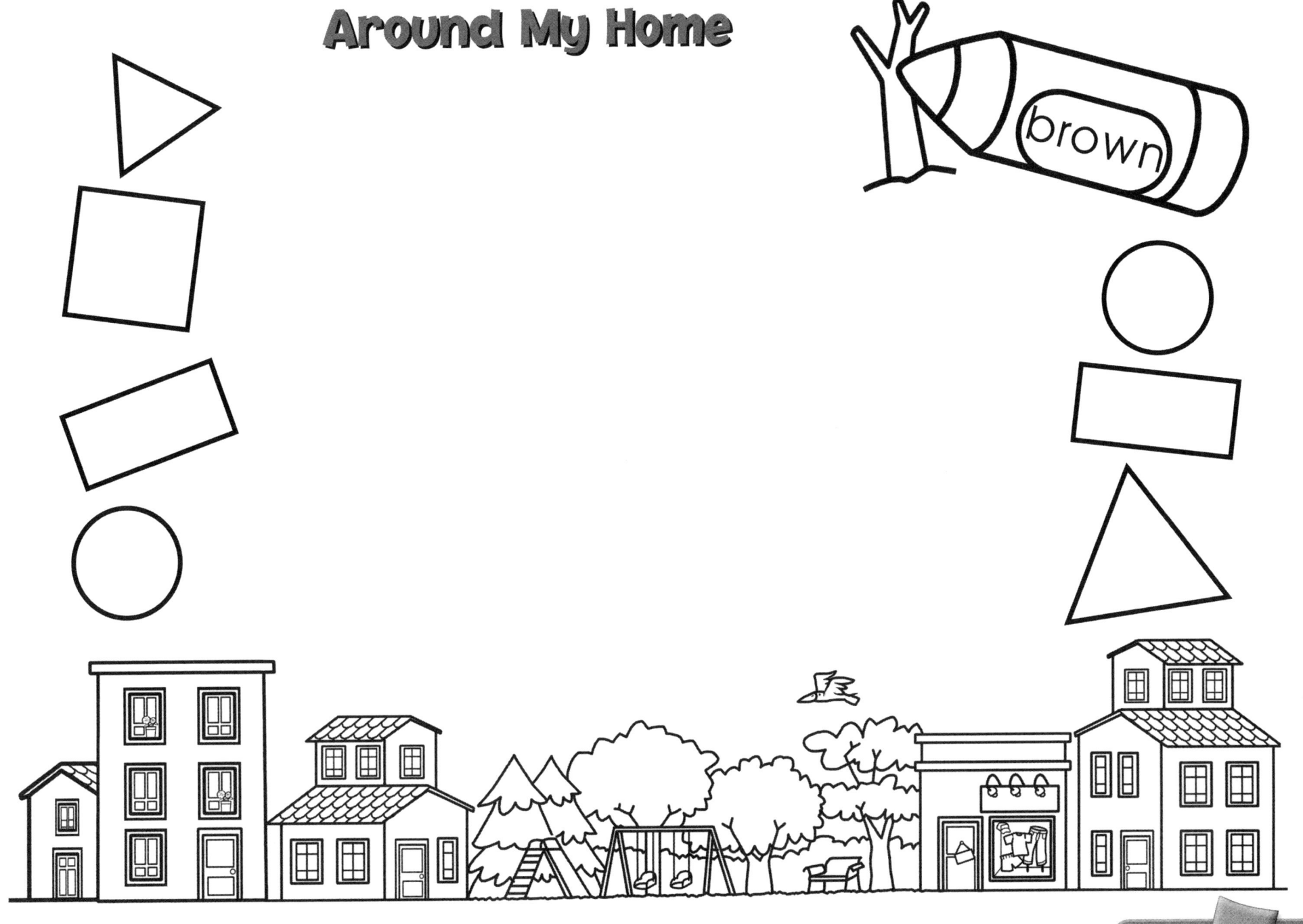

# Around My Home

brown

Point to the items and say. Draw your home.

**Assessment** Unit 8 65

# UNIT 9 Nature Around Us

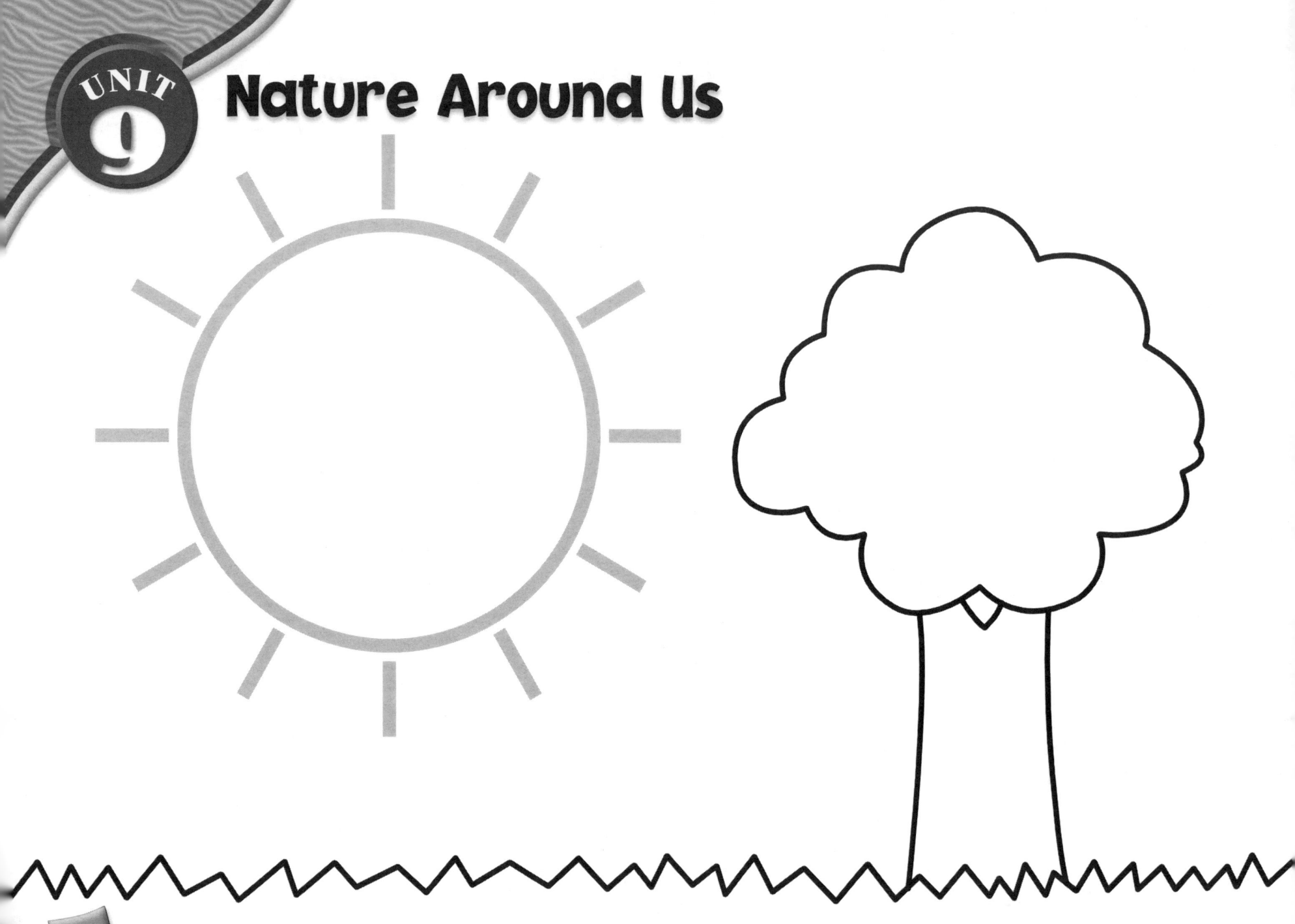

66 Unit 9 **Warm Up**

Trace and color the *sun*. Color the *tree* and *grass*.

Trace and color the *flower*. Color the *bugs* and *dirt*.

68 Unit 9  Practice

Trace and color the shapes. Point and say.

Draw *bugs*. Point and say. Color.

Practice Unit 9

70 Unit 9 Practice

Color the crayons. Color the items on the page.

Trace the *sun* and color.

Practice Unit 9 71

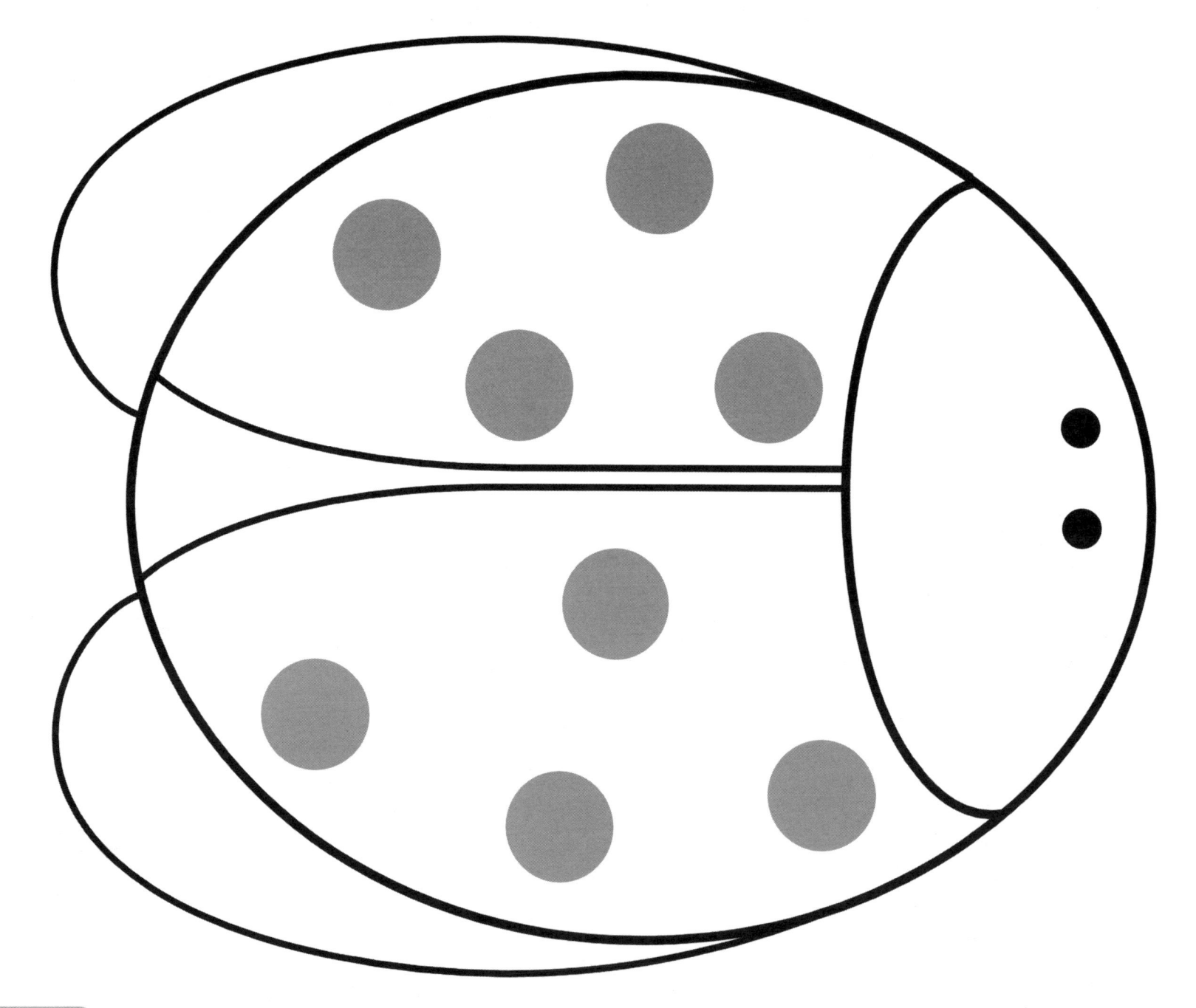

Paste paper or tissue on the *ladybug's* spots. Color.

# Nature Around Us

Point to the items and say. Draw a *tree*.

**Assessment** Unit 9 73

Color and cut out the puppet. Tape or glue the puppet to a stick.
Use the puppet for role-plays and conversations.

Puppet 75

**76** Puppet

Color and cut out the puppet. Tape or glue the puppet to a stick.
Use the puppet for role-plays and conversations.

_____

# has finished Cornerstone Pockets 1 Workbook.